Don't Just Start a Business
Build an Empire

How to See Beyond Entrepreneurship and Create a Game Plan for your Legacy

Gerald Washington

with Candice L. Davis

Don't Just Start a Business Build an Empire
How to See Beyond Entrepreneurship and Create a Game Plan for your Legacy
By Gerald Washington with Candice L. Davis

ISBN 978-0-9859080-4-1

Published by:
Seek Wisdom Find Wealth Publishing
Pasadena CA 91105

Contents

Thank You

I must start by thanking my amazing wife and bestfriend, Patrice. You have stuck by me through all the trying times, held my hand and head up when things were rough. You have always seen more in me than I see in myself. I love you and this empire is for you. To my father, my teacher and my rock your spirit will live on through these pages and our legacy. To my beautiful daughters, please know that everything I do is to ensure you have the launching pad I did not. Always stay focused on your dreams and build everyday. I love you. To my mother you have shown me the way a person should live their life and I pray each and every day I make you proud. To my sister Genea and my brother Haleefa you both have provided me the support that any brother would die for, I'll see you both at the top. And finally to anyone who has ever supported me, prayed for me, worked alongside me or simply smiled as I moved throughout life's journey, I thank you! It is my prayer that the words within change your life and help you see yourself as an empire builder too.

Gerald Washington

Becoming an Empire Builder

I made my first million dollars as an entrepreneur before I turned twenty-six years old. In college, I built a successful marketing company, which was profitable from day one. Later, I shut down to focus on real estate. That business brought in a lot more money, a lot faster. I saw annual revenues of more than $2 million, and partnered with the woman who would become my wife, I amassed an inventory of thirteen properties with multiple units. I took on team members and leased a large office space. I drove luxury cars and lived in a big house. If anyone tells you it takes a long time to get rich, you can point to me as living proof that the statement is only true if you let it be.

Before you start to think I must've had some kind of head start, let me tell you I wasn't born into money. In fact, I grew up in South Central Los Angeles, where everybody was hustling, living check to check, trying to figure out how to stretch a dollar just a little farther. My mother was a social worker, and my father was an animal control officer, good jobs that put us solidly in the middle class. We were always comfortable, but as a kid, my shoes came from Payless and I never lived in a home with more than one bathroom. I shared a bedroom with my younger sister, and when we were older and my younger brother came along, all three of us shared one room in our dad's apartment. The businesses I founded and grew in my twenties changed my lifestyle in very tangible ways. Unfortunately, that change didn't last.

Just five years after I established myself as a business success story, I lost more than that first million. I lost all of my money and my material assets—all the *stuff* that made me feel rich—and my real estate business folded. It had always been important to me to not only be a high performer but to also have the outward appearance of success. I wanted to look rich, and I did, but when the housing market crashed, all of those expensive things went away faster than I'd acquired them. My wife, Patrice, and I had to move our family out of our six thousand square foot house, in Los Angeles, California. We surrendered the matching Land Rovers we could no longer pay for and went from riding in luxury to driving one of the big yellow cargo vans we'd used for our construction business—not exactly a baller look.

With our young daughter strapped in her car seat and the few belongings we could take with us packed in the van, we drove across the country to Louisiana. We didn't want to leave L.A., where Patrice and I had lived all of our lives, but we'd run out of options. The three of us moved into a six hundred square foot apartment, in New Orleans, while I tried to squeeze a few dollars out of the few properties I still owned there. But the real estate boom, during which my wife and I had both done incredibly well, was over. The bubble had burst, and there was nothing left.

We didn't go from rich to middle class. Middle class implies a stable, sufficient income. We didn't have that. It implies a decent place to live and enough money to pay for electricity, heat, and water without having to choose which one you'll pay late. We didn't have that either. I needed to make some money fast, but so did the other eight million Americans who lost their jobs and the two hundred thousand who closed their businesses. In the face of layoffs, hiring freezes, crumbling corporations, and record unemployment, I did what I had to. I went from running a seven-figure real estate company to working at Taco Bell, the same place I'd worked before I was old enough to get a driver's license. I never expected to put that uniform on again, but I had to face reality. We had bills to pay and a child to feed.

The country was in the midst of the Great Recession and jobs were nearly impossible to come by. Companies much bigger than mine—multibillion dollar entities like General Motors, Fannie Mae, and Lehman Brothers—were going belly up. Huge banks and automakers were struggling and would end up needing the federal government (in other words, American taxpayers) to bail them out. Workers in every industry worried about getting laid off. People were desperate to hold on to their jobs for as long as they lasted, even when their annual salary increases disappeared. Working at Taco Bell was a blessing for me, but it was a hard blessing to receive. People can get surprisingly nasty when you forget the sour cream for their burritos.

Together, my wife and I started from zero, and slowly but consistently, over the next several years, we rebuilt. However, this time, we created something much stronger. As I write this, my wife has her own very successful business and a rewarding career as "America's Money Maven." She's the author of several books, an in-demand speaker, and respected a business strategist. For my part, I'm back in real estate in a big way. This comes on the heels of my work as executive producer on seven different television shows as a partner in a major production company. In that space, I also created and promoted major events, managed talent, and invested in other businesses. Today, I regularly negotiate and execute on multi-seven-figure deals, and my income well exceeds what I earned in my early days of entrepreneurship. And I'm ready for more.

Don't get me wrong. Our economic recovery didn't happen overnight. It took a lot of hard work, sacrifice, and discipline, but what I've built as I've grown and matured in business and in life far surpasses what I created in my twenties. This time around, I've laid a stronger foundation and I have a much clearer understanding of the limitless potential of what I can build. Nothing about this journey has been easy, but I'd take all those hits again to acquire the knowledge and wisdom I have now. It was worth the price because I finally understand what it takes to create wealth—not just make a lot of money—and I've gone from an entrepreneur to an empire builder.

I wrote *Don't Just Start a Business. Build an Empire!* to show you how you can make the same leap I've made—and do it faster than I did, with fewer hard mistakes. The time for playing at business is over. The stakes are too high. The kind of economic power too many of us have left untapped has the ability to change family legacies, lift whole communities out of poverty, alter the political landscape, and shape the future in ways that have been inconceivable for many of us for way too long.

The lie you've been told is that becoming an entrepreneur is the way to get everything you want. You've been told that starting a business puts you in control of your life. You've been told that ownership buys you freedom. However, far too many entrepreneurs get stuck in a trap of working for their business instead of creating a business that works for them. They put on a persona of "team no sleep" or # hustleandgrind like it's a badge of honor, and then they proceed to work eighty-hour weeks, neglect their families, and destroy their health for an enterprise that would fall apart if they failed to show up to work tomorrow.

Too many starry-eyed entrepreneurs create a business that's really just another job. Most don't earn any more than they could in the workforce, and even those who do typically make huge sacrifices in other areas of their lives to earn that money. They don't have passive income. They don't have an asset they can sell if they decide to pursue other interests or have an immediate need for cash. At the same time, they convince themselves they're free because they don't have a boss anymore. Yet, they work longer hours than any employer would expect them to work. They're clients and customers and even their employees dictate how these entrepreneurs will spend their time. They're trapped in a prison of their own making.

Here's the hard truth. If you really want freedom—time freedom and financial freedom—you have to go beyond entrepreneurship. Use it as a stepping stone, but hold a vision for something bigger. See yourself as an empire builder, and start taking action in that direction. When you build an empire, you not only create freedom for yourself and your family, you also multiply exponentially the positive impact and influence you can have on the business world, on your industry, on your community, and beyond.

If you've been thinking of going into business for yourself, but you haven't been able to figure out where to start, this book will help you decide if running a business is really the right path for you. It will show you how much bigger your dream can be. It doesn't matter if you were that kid who always had some kind of hustle, like I did, or you've always played it safe with the day job you once believed would offer you a lifetime of security. The principles in *Don't Just Start a Business. Build an Empire!* will help you jump into business the smart way, always with an eye on your future empire. If you apply what you learn here from the beginning, you'll avoid a lot of common pitfalls. The Rookie Action Steps I share in each chapter are for you.

The guiding principles for running a successful, highly profitable business never change, no matter how long you're at it. If you've been in business for a while and you're looking to increase your profits, grow your business, or start a new venture, the principles in this book can help you do all of that. They can help you take the next step and become an empire builder. The Veteran Action Steps are for you.

If you've been in business for a while, and you're wondering if you qualify as a veteran yet, then consider yourself a rookie and take action on both the rookie and the veteran steps as they apply to you. This book cannot hold your hand and do the work for you. If you read about a specific strategy, and it doesn't have a specific action step associated with it, but you know you need to do something, do it. Don't wait for someone to tell you what to apply and when to apply it. If you want that kind of micromanaging, you need to hang on to your day job.

Becoming successful in business means doing the work, every day, day after day, week after week, month after month—even when it's not easy, even when you don't feel like it. Winning in business means getting back up, ready to play again, when you get knocked down. If you're committed to making it happen, if you're willing to challenge what you've up until now believed to be true and apply what you learn, you can build a profitable business, and you can go from successful business owner to empire builder.

The challenge to think bigger and differently can be intimidating, especially if you're just getting started or you're struggling every day to figure out how to make payroll or just keep the office lights on. Don't get caught up in what you don't know or haven't done yet. Instead, dive into the principles I share here. Open your mind to new possibilities, well beyond what you once thought could happen for you. Position yourself to exceed all expectations, including your own. Don't settle for being an entrepreneur. Become an empire builder.

Wealth requires
sustainability,
and sustainability
takes time.

1

Think Like an Empire Builder

You can't take a financial hit like the one my family and I took without feeling it. Together, my wife and I had created a mini real estate empire, and with the crash of the housing market, in 2008, we'd lost it all. Living in survival mode takes a toll on you physically, emotionally, and mentally. Even though I kept fighting to get us back on our feet, I really was knocked off my game. My confidence, which had a certain amount of cockiness too, was shook. I honestly hadn't seen any of the economic disaster coming. The money, the properties, the big house, the fancy office, the luxury cars—all of the material representations of success were gone. Fortunately, I still had my work ethic, my belief in my ability to do what few are willing to do and create exceptional income, and the support of my wife to keep me moving forward.

So yes, I went back to work at Taco Bell, my old after-school job. It was a huge blow to my ego. I went from a suite of private offices to the drive-thru, from wearing a suit to putting on a uniform, and from calling the shots to putting up with abusive customers so I could bring home a paycheck. There I was, a thirty-year-old African American man, a husband and father with a degree from a prestigious private college, and I was slinging fast food. I spent my days arguing with people who saw me as undeserving of basic respect because I was, in their eyes, just a fast food worker. I came home every day smelling like ground beef and onions. It was humbling and exhausting. Had I gone into debt to get a private college education, invested so much time and energy in building a business, and worked so hard to end up right back behind the counter of a fast food restaurant. No. That was my reality at that moment, but I kept my eyes open for the next opportunity.

When *The Steve Harvey Morning Show* came to New Orleans for an event my wife suggested we go down and say hello. She had interned on the radio show while she was in college, and she wanted to reconnect. I put on a suit, and Patrice put on a nice dress, and we went down to greet the cast. It was worth the effort. My wife came out of that reunion with a job prospect. It wasn't her dream job, but it gave her the chance to relocate to Atlanta, where she and Reagan would live with Patrice's brother, and she could start bringing in some money again.

Not long after my wife and daughter left Louisiana, I was evicted from our apartment, so I slept on a mattress in the basement of one of our upside-down properties—no furniture, no television, no hot water. Later, I transferred to a Taco Bell in Atlanta and joined my family. We had no clue at the time, but that move would eventually become the entry point for me to build a successful career in the entertainment industry.

Business has its ups and downs. There will be setbacks and deals that fall through. There may even be a major crisis or two. If we had given in to depression and embarrassment, we would never have gone to the event that proved to be a turning point for us. If we had doubted our ability to change our situation for the better, we wouldn't have shown up with the right attitude. I knew my wife and I both still had all of the same skills that had allowed us to earn great money in the past. I wasn't sure how we would do it, but I saw a future in which we had all that we had lost and more.

It wasn't always easy, but we were determined to think like winners as we rebuilt. We believed in our gifts and abilities and our willingness to work for what we wanted. When the time came, that mental preparedness made it possible for us to step into opportunities and make the most of them. I eventually landed a job as a production assistant, essentially the lowest man on the totem pole in the entertainment world, and worked my way up to an executive producer for several television programs. That achievement paved the way for me to jump back into business for myself.

Only a fool would show up for a championship game out of shape and unprepared, and your mental game is a big part of that readiness. If you want to win in business, you need to develop the mindset of a winner. You need to condition yourself to face the challenges that will inevitably come. What you believe will determine what you achieve. Your mental conditioning is a must for continued success and growth in your business. If you want to go from employee to entrepreneur, you have to make that mindset shift, and when you're ready to go from entrepreneur to empire builder, you'll need to level up your mindset once again. How long it takes to go from one level to the next is up to you.

I want to challenge you to start thinking like an empire builder now, wherever you are in this process. Push yourself to see beyond your job, beyond your first business launch, beyond what you've been told to expect from entrepreneurship. If you don't think like an empire builder, you're definitely not going to act like one, and you won't get the results you want. You have to go into business determined to win, with a clear understanding of what that means to you, and a vision for how you'll go from entrepreneur to empire builder.

Whatever you're setting out to accomplish, you have to believe it's possible for you, commit one hundred percent to the work required, and be willing to continue to learn along the way. Over years of working for myself and with other high-achieving business owners, I've developed a set of core beliefs that contribute to my success.

Empire-Builder Belief #1: You are a born entrepreneur— and you can make the leap to empire builder.

People who work generally fall into one of three categories:

1. Employees
2. Entrepreneurs
3. Empire builders

Employees have no real desire for ownership. Even if they're high performers, they don't see themselves as owners because they typically value the *feeling* of security they get from employment above all else. They prefer the known to the unknown, even when the known isn't all that great. The best employees provide a great support system for entrepreneurs and empire builders. They're the front lines of our businesses. Most people, from food service workers to executives, fall into this category.

Entrepreneurs recognize that they can create something of value on their own. They're willing to take some amount of initiative and risk and to do what it takes to build a business and compete in the marketplace, but they stop there. Most often, they end up working for their business rather than their business working for them. Whether it's $100,000 a year or $10,000,000 a year, their business structure puts a ceiling on what the entrepreneur can earn.

Empire builders are a different breed. We have a bigger, broader vision, and even if we don't know how exactly we'll get there, we're willing to learn along the way and figure it out. We set ourselves apart by doing what other business owners won't do. We're willing to take bigger risks for bigger payoffs, and when things go wrong, we don't give up. Empire builders find another way because we recognize that there is no ceiling on what we can earn and no limit on the positive impact we can have. As an empire builder, your success won't be defined by a specific dollar amount. Instead, it will be defined by multiple and diversified streams of income, the fact that you're no longer trading hours for dollars, and the reach and influence of your empire.

The world needs employees. Entrepreneurs and empire builders couldn't exist without them. They're your team, your support system, the people executing your plans on the front lines and in the management offices. Entrepreneurs also play a key role in our communities. We all have our favorite local restaurants, coffee shops, cigar bars, salons, and barbershops that are run by entrepreneurs. Some business owners are satisfied operating at this level, and that's fine. However, many entrepreneurs are stuck there because they don't see how they can leverage their resources to do more. They don't believe they can, and so they shortchange themselves, their families, and the world by failing to make the most of their full potential.

Before you can become an empire builder you have to believe you can be successful in business. The fact is that winning in business is possible for everyone at some level because we're all entrepreneurs at heart. It doesn't matter what your background is or how much experience you do or do not have in business. You're a natural-born entrepreneur. I say this because, like everyone else, you have a gift you can tap into and monetize by creating value for people who are willing and able to pay you for it. The only question is whether or not you're willing to do the work to make it happen.

If you have an MBA, a business degree, or any kind of college degree, that's great, but you don't need any of that to become a successful entrepreneur. Whether you know it or not, you already have many of the necessary skills. You can learn whatever else you need to know or hire someone to handle those tasks for you. The best way to develop an entrepreneurial mindset and a belief in your ability to succeed is to start acting like an entrepreneur right now, right where you are. That's a great first step and often necessary before you can see yourself as an empire builder.

If you work for someone else, you can flex your entrepreneurial skills in your current job. If you're doing the job you were hired to do, then you already invest your time and your talents into the company. Treat the company like a partner. Go in and give your employer your best effort every day just like you would your own business. Within your scope of influence, take initiative, offer solutions, and identify opportunities for improvement. An effective leader will recognize the value you create. You'll be rewarded for your contributions while you strengthen the muscles you need to succeed out on your own.

If you feel driven to become a business owner, you have to see yourself as the entrepreneur you were born to be. There's no benchmark you need to hit to deserve that title. Recognize that any additional skills or information you need to be successful in this arena you can get. In the meantime, claim your birthright, and start acting like the entrepreneur you want to become. And then reach for more. Trust that you can make the leap from entrepreneur to empire builder.

Empire-Builder Belief #2:
It takes time to become wealthy, but you can make money fast.

I started making good money at such a young age that I never saw creating income as a difficult thing to do. Because of that belief and my willingness to take action with my gift for bringing people together to have a good time, I made money fast. My event marketing program was a thriving enterprise right up to the point when I closed it to jump into real estate. Each home sale was a transaction worth hundreds of thousands of dollars, and I figured out how to get as much of that for myself as I could. Before long, I was rich by most people's standards.

Getting rich simply requires you to ma a lot of money, and that's something that can happen fast. You probably know someone in your life or in the media who got rich seemingly overnight. In the blink of an eye, pro athletes get drafted and go from a childhood home in the hood to a mansion behind the gates. Some new hip hop star has a hit, and the next thing you know that star is travelling with an entourage and flying on private jets. They're rich, but that doesn't mean they're wealthy. Wealth requires sustainability, and sustainability takes time. Building an empire—instead of stopping at building a business—is essential to long-term success and wealth building.

Since my first go at business, I've learned to define a wealthy life in new ways. Following my wife's philosophy, I've redefined wealth to include my physical and mental fitness, relationships, lifestyle, faith, and the freedom to live my life's purpose. There is no true success without a measure of success in all of these areas. But when it comes to money, I define wealth as financial sustainability created through the accumulation of valuable assets and the know-how to continue to accumulate more, not just money in the bank or on paper. Unlike fast money, wealth creation requires life experience and knowledge. You can get rich chasing money, but wealth comes from a long-term practice of earning, spending, saving, and investing wisely.

That being said, don't allow anyone to tell you that you have to pay your dues and climb the ladder one rung at a time or that you have to wait years to earn a lot money in business. Instead, figure out how you can make money quickly while you develop the insight and discernment to become wealthy over time.

Empire-Builder Belief #3:
Businesses should fund themselves.

I love creating events and bringing people together to have a good time. As a college student, event marketing was work that excited me, and I still keep a hand in that line of business. In 2017, I worked with a business partner to create a five-day event in the Bahamas. As I put the event together, I brought on strategic partners, who provided products and services. Even though it was the first time it was held, the event was profitable for us before the first guest arrived. It turned out to be a huge success. However, as good as it looked on paper and as much fun as it promised to be, I would have pulled the plug on the whole thing if it wasn't going to pay for itself and create a significant profit.

A lot of entrepreneurs get so excited about their products or services or about the idea of being their own boss that they forget the fundamental purpose of a business: ***to make money***. You need to start with a profitability mindset from the very beginning. Depending on what industry you're in and how much time and money you have to invest, you may find you're immediately profitable or that it takes several months to get there, but ***profit is always the goal***.

You hear exciting success stories about companies that started in a dorm room, went years without making any money, and eventually blew up into the next biggest thing. These stories are usually from the tech industry, and one of the most common examples people like to toss around is Facebook, which didn't make a profit for the first five years. But Facebook had a long-term plan. More importantly, the company had investor money to keep it going while the plan was executed.

Most small businesses will never be chosen by angel investors or venture capitalists to receive an infusion of funds. No one's going to knock on your door and offer you a big check for a percentage of your company. It costs money to run a business—even a small business—and you have to figure out how to raise that capital on your own. The best way to do that is to require your business to fund itself. In order to make that happen, you have to keep your expenses low enough that you can cover them with the money you earn.

Let's take the example of an auto mechanic who wants to open his own shop. He needs to ask himself a few questions before he goes out and signs that lease or buys a garage:

1. How many cars does he work on in his home garage every month?
2. How much money is he already making from auto repairs?

3. Is it enough money to cover the additional overhead?
4. Do people in his community know and trust his work?
5. Are his services already in demand?
6. Does he have the ability to identify and hire the technicians and office workers he'll need?
7. How long will it take him to bring in enough money every month to cover the lease, utilities, taxes, insurance, payroll, and other business expenses?
8. And how much money will be left for his own salary every month?

You'll likely need some start-up capital to launch your business, but you should earn that money through your day job. If you don't have the money on hand, then you're not ready to start this business. You either need to continue to work and save or consider a different opportunity. If you've got the money set aside and ready to go, you need to jump into that business with a commitment to get profitable as quickly as you can. Your business should be paying its own bills.

If the business can't pay for new laptops, you don't get new laptops yet. If the business can't cover the costs of office space, you work from home or from a co-working space. Plenty of successful businesses have been built from a laptop at a table in a Starbucks. Remember you're in business to make money, not to sink deeper and deeper into debt. *Your business needs to fund itself.* When you make this a founding principle and set that expectation, you'll find it easy to make the kinds of decisions that will support your goal of becoming an empire builder.

I'm often asked by new business owners whether or not they should borrow money to launch a business or do a deal. I believe in using OPP, or other people's money, to run a business. If you're confident in your idea, you've tested it, and you're passionate about it, then you might consider that as an option. However, understand that if your business fails, that debt doesn't go away. You're personally responsible for it. That money should be an investment in your business, not a way to cover your personal expenses. Never use money borrowed for your business to finance your lifestyle. Work your job for that. When your business is profitable and can cover both the loan repayment and your lifestyle, then you can quit your job.

Rookie Action Step

Make a decision now. Are you more comfortable as an employee, or are you looking for more? Are you willing lay the foundation, take the risks, and work to build your empire? Employee, entrepreneur, or empire builder—commit now to which one you plan to be and get ready to do the work.

Veteran Action Step

Take a hard look at your business. Is your business self-funding? Can your business earn money even when you (the owner) aren't working? Have you figured out how to make money fast while reinvesting to create future wealth? Are you building something that will leave a tangible legacy?

If you answered *yes* to all of those questions, congratulations. You're on your way to becoming an empire builder. Keep reading and apply the strategies in the following chapters to make sure you make that potential a reality. If you answered *no* to some or all of those questions, you've got work to do, but it can be done. Read on.

Find opportunities to make the most of who and what you already know—and what you're known for.

2

Lay the Foundation for Your Empire

On the road to reclaiming our own financial power, my wife landed a job with a non-profit organization with a mission of economic empowerment. Patrice started off as a volunteer, but she already had years of experience conducting her own personal finance workshops for people who wanted to prepare to buy a home. She'd always had a passion for teaching financial literacy, and she quickly demonstrated that she had deeper knowledge and skills that would benefit the organization. The higher-ups wisely offered her a permanent paid position. In her new job, she was able to make significant improvements in the organization while doing something she loved. During that time, Patrice also saw an opportunity to make the most of her knowledge by putting it in a book. She had a vision for how that book could open doors for her to build a new business. Together, we began to have a little more clarity about how we could get out of our dire financial straits a little faster. I encouraged her to follow her vision.

My wife recognized that her knowledge and her gift for sharing it were the keys to creating more income for herself than she could ever earn in that job. Writing her first book would help her reach tens of thousands of people with a message of hope and practical strategies for money management. It would position her as the expert in her field. It would change her life for the better in ways we couldn't begin to predict. Unfortunately, her employers were not as excited about this opportunity as we were. A company wide email was issued shortly after her release, affirming "If anyone creates financial education content of any kind, we own it."

The argument was that any intellectual property an employee created, even on her own time, belonged to the company. But we saw things differently. If they had offered to even partner with her in publishing and promoting her book, Patrice would certainly have been willing to come up with an arrangement that served everyone involved. I was working as an assistant, a very junior position, and we needed the income. I was standing in the middle of a kitchen renovation at my boss's house, when Patrice called me to tell me about the email. I looked around at the success he'd managed to achieve. It was impressive, but it was also a reminder of the fact that my wife and I had just as much potential. I told Patrice to quit her job.

We immediately cut back on our spending and started saving more money. I began to hustle a little differently on my job, and we saved two months of my take-home pay to have as a cushion. Patrice looked for opportunities to share her gift for personal finance, money management, and increasing income. She created a plan that allowed her to start earning money from her business right away, giving her time and space to write her second book. In the first month after she quit her job with the non-profit, she had people signed up to do a webinar and for mini coaching sessions. Within the first month—in fact, within the first couple of days that she was back in business for herself—my wife was already out-earning what the non-profit had paid her.

If you're just thinking about starting your own business, you actually have an advantage over many people who are already deep into the process. You still have time to do all of the preparation that can give your business the best chance of succeeding. The principles in this chapter will help you set yourself up for success right out of the gate. If you're already running your business, this is your chance to make sure you've laid the proper groundwork for success.

Allow your job to finance your business launch.

Unless you're sitting on a large sum of cash, by which I mean two or three years' worth of income separate and apart from what you need to start your business, you need to position yourself for your job to fund your business. Yes, you want your business to be profitable as soon as possible so it can fund itself, but most businesses don't make money right away. That means you have to set aside some of your current income, after you've paid your living expenses, to finance your business. In the beginning, you need to go to your job from nine to five and work at your business from five to nine until you work yourself out of that day job and your business is ready to self-fund.

It can be exciting to go after your dream of being a business owner, especially once you recognize that it's just the start of building your empire. There's nothing sexier than working for yourself, and I encourage you to do it. But don't be a fool. You can't just get an idea in your head and quit your job to pursue it. When you jump out there with no financial safety net and no income, you put your personal financial security and your family's financial well-being at unnecessary risk. But if you build your business in your off hours, while you continue to collect your regular paycheck, you can move forward confident that your basic needs will be met regardless of how your business does.

According to the U.S. Small Business Administration, half of all businesses with employees fail to make it to year five. Sometimes the owner closes the doors on a business for reasons other than a lack of profitability, but the bottom line is that once a business closes, the business owner no longer has that income to depend on. No one starts a business with a plan to fail. Everyone thinks they're going to be one of the fifty percent of people who make it work. But fifty percent of you are wrong.

At the same time, only forty percent of small businesses are profitable. If you think working for someone else for a paycheck is tough, imagine working long hours for yourself and still not being able to pay your bills. As I learned when I had to go back to working at Taco Bell after losing my real estate business, scrambling to get a job when you're desperate for money because your business fails to generate income is a bad position to put yourself in. If you leave your job because you have pie-in-the-sky ideas about the salary your new business will pay you, you can expect to find yourself in a similar position.

It's unreasonable to expect your family to sacrifice lifestyle and comfort so you can pursue your business dreams. If you have a spouse, children, or anyone else depending on you, they shouldn't have to lower their quality of life so you can quit your job and go after your business goals. Even if you're single and child-free, somebody has to pay the rent. Depending on your spouse, your parents, or anyone else to provide for you financially while you figure out how

Preparation for
failure offers
increased
opportunity
for success.

to successfully run a business is an unfair burden to place on the people who love you. You have to take responsibility for financing your dream.

It's incredibly challenging for most people to save up the equivalent of two to three years' worth of salary (again, *in addition to* whatever cash you need to finance your business). Unless you get some kind of windfall, like a significant inheritance or a huge severance package, stashing that amount of cash at once might be impossible in your current situation. That's why you need to hold on to your day job until your business is showing a consistent profit and providing enough income for you to maintain your lifestyle on the salary your business pays you. Whether you need to cut back on personal expenses, get a second job for a while, or find a way to earn a raise on your current job, your salary needs to pay for your living expenses first and your business second.

When you're launching a business, the security of knowing your mortgage will be paid, there'll be food on the table, and your lights and your Wi-Fi will be on at the end of the day will give you much-needed confidence. You won't have to make decisions out of fear or desperation. You won't have to take on high-maintenance clients or discount your products or services just to get a few dollars coming in. You'll be able to assess opportunities much more clearly when you know your mortgage will be paid whether a particular deal goes through or not.

If you have a family, that kind of stability is even more important because your ability to pay the bills impacts your spouse and your children in a very real way. If you're single, you might be able to significantly reduce your personal overhead, but you don't want to sacrifice all of your quality of life or end up moving from couch to couch because you failed to get your business profitable quickly enough. Keep your day job until you can consistently and completely replace your nine-to-five income with the income you draw from your business.

If you've already left your job to start a business, but you aren't bringing home enough money to do your part in supporting your family or paying your own personal overhead, it's not too late. There's an easy fix to that problem. *Get a damn job.* That's not a sign of failure. That's a sign of responsibility. It's a demonstration that you're serious about becoming a successful business owner, and you're willing to do whatever it takes to get there. Put your pride aside. There's no emotion in business just money. Empire builders recognize that short-term sacrifices, like working a job while you build that first business, are often the best way to long-term gains.

While you're at work, give your employer one hundred percent of your attention and your effort. Figure out how to be efficient and effective at your job so you have time and energy left for your business, but don't short-change your boss. Be in integrity wherever you are, including on your nine-to-five. Stealing time or resources from your boss is the opposite of acting in integrity, and it's not the foundation you want to build your future on. Imagine you're the business owner and you discover your employees are using the time you're paying them for to start a side business. They would essentially be stealing from you, and you would be wise to let them go. So would your boss.

Yes, allowing your job to finance your business means you'll essentially have two (or even three) jobs for a while. You won't be able to come home at the end of the day and crash on the couch in front of the television. Your social life will probably be non-existent, and getting in some family time might mean you work on your business after the kids go to bed or while you're sitting on the side-lines at the soccer field. Building a business while you work for someone else at the same time requires commitment, dedication, and sacrifice—just like running your business full-time will. This is a great time to build your endurance and figure out how to best manage your time while the risks are low.

My wife and I have taken this principle a step farther. We were both entrepreneurs when we started our relationship. Unfortunately, in the beginning, we built businesses in the same industry. The housing crisis hit and the real estate market crashed during our engagement. We'd both gambled on the housing market to stay strong for years to come, and we both lost. My wife was much more savvy about money management than I was at the time. Before our marriage, she had saved where I had spent, so she had a safety net. But ultimately, we were in business together, and we didn't have either the reserves or the diversification to survive the extreme shift in the housing market.

When our business finally folded, we were financially devastated. Later, we agreed that we would never fully invest our work and business interests in the same industry again. There's just too much risk involved. As we learned the hard way, when an entire industry takes a hit, it can take years to recover. Part of building an empire is diversifying your income sources so you can weather a downturn in one area while another continues to profit. In addition to diversifying our careers, we also agreed that one of us will always hold down a job outside of our own businesses.

While Patrice and I will never trust one industry to provide all of our income again, we've evolved past the "day job" rule. I still think it's a good rule for many people, but the fact is that I can make significantly more money working for myself than I can working for someone else. Even if a company pays me six figures, whatever salary they commit to pay me places a ceiling on what I can earn, and I'd have to work within company structures and guidelines and report to someone every day. I know I can easily make $350,000 a year without doing all of that. Just as importantly, working for myself removes all limits from my earning potential. A day job with a set salary offers me no challenge and it doesn't allow me to build my empire the way I want to, at the pace I want to build it. We're fortunate to be in the position to make this decision, but a two-entrepreneur household is definitely not for beginners.

Allowing your job to finance your business requires a lot more discipline than just quitting your nine-to-five and trying to figure out your business as you go along. It requires you to work hard at your job all day and come home and work hard on your business in the evening and on weekends. It means that, for a period of time, your business will take up most of your free time. But that's the smart way to play this game, *and the day you're able to quit your job or just allow that paycheck to come in, knowing you don't really need it, is the day you'll know you've won.*

See the opportunities other people miss.

In my senior year at Junipero Serra High School, I started a business venture that turned out to be quite profitable—but not for me. One day, I noticed our school had a cookie machine that was just sitting there, gathering dust, and I saw dollar signs. The school didn't sell any kind of dessert, so I knew kids would be happy to spend some of their lunch money or their allowance to get a midday sugar fix. I promised Mr. Pilato, my school principal, that, if he allowed me to use the machine to make cookies and sell them to students, I'd turn over all of the profits to the school. (See any problems with that deal?)

Of course, our principal was no fool, and it sounded like a winning proposition to him. He gave me permission to use the machine during my free period, which conveniently enough was just before lunch. I put up my own money to pay for the cookie

You have to be willing to put in the work and own the results.

dough, and it was on. I baked and sold ten dozen cookies every day, and at a price of a dollar per cookie, my little business generated a nice profit. How many other people, whether students or faculty or staff, had seen that machine sitting there and looked right past it? Maybe a few of them thought it might be a good idea to put it to use, but it didn't matter. I was the one who saw it as an opportunity and moved on it.

The ability to recognize an opportunity and the willingness to act on it served me well, sort of. Unfortunately, I'd been short-sighted and too eager to strike a deal in my negotiation with the principal. I recognized my mistake too late. I was doing all the work and I put up all the money, but I had promised to give the school all of the profits. With the immature thinking of a teenager, I decided I would just pocket the money I'd made. After all, I was graduating and would be moving on from high school. In the grand scheme of things, it wasn't a lot of money, and I reasoned that no one would really notice or care. However, Mr. Pilato had a different opinion, and he had some important leverage I'd failed to consider. He refused to release my diploma until I turned over the cash.

Even though I obviously went about the cookie business the wrong way, my ability to recognize an opportunity and go after it has always served me well. I knew I didn't have to reinvent the wheel to add value. I didn't have to search outside of my day-to-day life to find an opportunity worth pursuing. Right in front of me, I had a captivated consumer base and a venture with no overhead and no expenses except the purchase of the product.

When you're looking for a business opportunity, there are usually plenty right in front of your face. You just have to see them. It could be an existing venture that you can participate in or partner with, or you might notice an untapped resource like the one I found. One of the easiest ways to find new business opportunities is to identify a problem that people are willing to pay to have solved. If everyone in your neighborhood complains about having to drive an hour to find a decent salon, then a brick-and-mortar salon, a team of mobile stylists, or a local space where stylists can rent out their own mini-salons could solve that problem for them.

What does your community need? What do you see people on social media complaining about or wishing they could find? Look at the places where you do business. Is there some way you can add value to what they do or do it better? Your employer probably has a budget for contractors and consultants. How can you get some of that money for yourself either through your current employer or from similar companies?

Practice the skill of noticing what other people miss. When you see a problem, come up with ways to solve it. Find an implementable solution that allows you to put your gifts to work creating value for the marketplace.

Plan for success.

Identifying an opportunity is essential, but it's just the beginning. Don't try to turn an idea into a business without a written plan. Your business plan is your playbook for success, a guide to take you from start to finish. Your plan needs to answer two essential questions: 1) What? 2) And by when? Spell out exactly what steps you or your team members will take to bring your plan to fruition and by what date you expect each task to be accomplished. It's that simple.

A lot of the business plan templates you'll find online or in books are overly complicated. I've started and run several successful businesses, and I've never written that kind of formal, complex business plan. You don't need a document designed in Harvard Business School. At this point, you are the primary audience for your business plan, so it needs to be something you and your team can understand and implement. That doesn't require a thirty-page presentation with slides, charts, and footnotes.

Your plan needs to include your offensive strategy and your defensive strategy for launching and running your business. There are several steps you need to take to create a strong offense:

1. Identify the opportunities for your business to generate income.
2. Decide what products or services you'll provide and how.
3. Figure out how many streams of income you can generate from each product or service.
4. Describe how you'll get your product in front of the right customers.
5. Forecast how much money you expect to make.
6. Forecast how fast you expect to make that amount of money.
7. Identify potential partners.
8. Identify what team members you need to execute your plan and achieve your goals.

Your defensive strategy, on the other hand, covers how you will protect your business from taking the kind of hits that can cost you money. While your specific industry will determine some of the defensive strategies you need to employ as a part of your plan, here are basic strategies every business owner needs to know, including:

1. Do your research, and become an expert on your industry.
2. Understand the common reasons similar businesses fail and take steps to avoid those pitfalls.
3. Diversify your income streams as soon as possible
4. Study past and current industry trends.
5. Forecast future market trends.
6. Avoid over-leveraging (taking on too much debt).

7 Create an exit strategy before you launch.
8 Remove the emotion from your decision-making process.
9 Avoid hiring family and friends.

If you aren't prepared for the things that can go wrong outside of your immediate control, it won't matter how good you are at what you do. When you have a full awareness of the variables that can impact your business, you can take action to prevent potential losses before they occur.

While your plan needs to cover both offense and defense, I always try to prepare more heavily for my defensive game. Preparation for failure offers increased opportunity for success. When you can see the negatives before they come at you, then you can counter them and turn them into positives. However, if you're so busy taking care of the offense that you forget to play defense, you'll get trapped every time. I'm not suggesting you hedge your bets out of fear of failure. In fact, if you don't believe you can win, then you shouldn't be playing the game of business. A strong defense simply positions you for the best possible offensive game.

As a young entrepreneur, I was like so many others. I was so focused on the flash and dazzle of my offensive game, that I left myself open to problems I never thought would affect me. My weak defensive strategy was the reason I lost my real estate business. I shut down my successful event marketing business and jumped into real estate because I saw how lucrative it could be. I was twenty-three years old, and I'd just bought my first home, one year after graduating from college, from the woman who would become my wife. I thought I wanted to get away, to get out of the hood, but my new house was an hour and a half away from everyone and everything I knew. My father warned me I'd never go out there to the suburbs, and he was right. I liked the idea of owning a home, but I had no use for one so far away from where my life was. I got as far as painting one wall, but I never even furnished the place.

That home purchase wasn't my best decision ever, but I kept the house for a couple of years and made about a hundred thousand dollars when I sold it. Recently, I bought a duplex on the street where I grew up, which in hindsight, I should have done the first time around. I could've lived in one unit while my dad took the other. Instead, I'd gotten caught up in the notion of the single family home with a garage in a nice neighborhood. It was supposed to be the American dream. Ultimately, I chose a house based on emotion.

While I hadn't thought my home purchase all the way through, that transaction opened my eyes to a new opportunity to make large sums of money. I saw the five-figure commission check Patrice got out of the deal, and I wanted some of that for myself. I'd never had any great passion for real estate, but I had a passion for making money. I was confident I could use my gift for negotiation and my experience in marketing to be successful in any industry. The smart move would've been to find a way to continue to run my event marketing business as I expanded into real estate. That way I would've maintained diversified income streams.

As it turned out, I did have transferable skills that helped me win in real estate while the market was good, but I was completely unprepared for the downturn. I hadn't researched the industry. I didn't keep up with the news, so I couldn't forecast where the trends were going. I didn't realize that, given the changes on the horizon, I was buying over-leveraged property. I had no exit plan. If I'd just turned on the morning news or picked up the business section of a newspaper, I would've seen that the market was headed in the wrong direction and the country was on the brink of the Great Recession.

In the end, that rush to get in on something that looked good on the surface cost me big. These days, I keep a close eye on industry trends and on the economy as a whole.

Another defensive strategy I employ is to remove the emotion from business. This was one of the biggest lessons of my early life as an entrepreneur, and it came from my uncle when I asked him to loan me $100,000. I'd found what I thought was a great deal on a twenty-three-station beauty salon. The property included a beauty supply store and a snack stand, and the owner was tired of running it. I went to my uncle, who I always saw as rich, with a thorough business plan. I asked for the loan, and he told me no.

My Uncle Tabb was the man who first opened my eyes to the possibility that I could have more than a comfortable, middle-class life. While he and my father both owned businesses, money was never a top priority for my dad. But my uncle was different. He owned a single-family house just a couple of miles from where we lived, and he traveled more than anyone else I knew. He always had more than one car, and when I was in elementary school, he even installed a car phone in his truck. He had a different style of communication and a different style of dress from the average man in my neighborhood because he aspired for more. He was the person who inspired me to reach higher, so when he turned me down, it hurt.

I was heartbroken, but my uncle was wisely protecting his money first. He refused to get caught up in my emotions or our relationship. The fact was that neither one of us knew anything about the beauty industry. I was still in my early twenties, and I didn't have the experience or wisdom to recognize that the salon might have been a great opportunity for someone, but it wasn't a business I needed to be in. His refusal to loan me the money seemed like a loss to me at the time, but it was a smart decision on my uncle's part and one of the most valuable lessons he could impart to me.

Every business needs a specific deadline by which it will succeed or shut down.

Just like the quarterback gets all the glory on the football field, offensive strategies can seem like the exciting part of business. After all, that's how the money's made. Playing defense for your business may not be as exciting, but it's just as important. A strong defense can mean the difference between protecting what you've created and invested in and losing it all.

Take fast action.

When I see an opportunity, I do my due diligence and I either decide to pass or move on it. I don't take blind risks, but I make decisions quickly. Some transactions will take longer to negotiate and execute, but I don't hesitate to make the decision of what to pursue, and I take action to do it fast. I can't afford to get caught up in spending a lot of time wondering if there might be something better out there or not—and neither can you. The bottom line is that if you don't move on a great opportunity, someone else will.

The primary reason I suggest you allow your job to fund your business in the beginning is to minimize your financial risks. When you reduce those risks, you also minimize your fear of failure because you don't have the full weight of your financial survival riding on your new venture. That security allows you to take more chances. Even if everything goes wrong and your business fails, you'll still be able to keep a roof over your head. But when you don't have that certainty, you'll worry about how you spend every dollar for your business. When it could mean the difference between paying your mortgage and losing your home, you'll tend to operate from a place of constant fear. That fear can make you second-guess every decision and keep you paralyzed.

Whether you're just getting started in your business or trying to choose your next move, it's easy to spend all your time researching or getting other people's opinions because you're too afraid to take responsibility for whatever might go wrong. The psychology behind so many of my "Prepare to Play" principles is to minimize your chances of failure so you can develop the confidence to take fast action. When you're scared, you're more likely to either make bad decisions or procrastinate so long that the decisions get made for you. Taking fast action isn't about jumping out there before you've done what it takes to get ready. It's about consistently moving toward your goal of a highly profitable business.

If you consistently procrastinate in your business, you have to ask yourself why. Is it just because you're lazy? If so, call it what it is. If laziness is preventing you from aggressively moving forward, be honest with yourself. You don't really want a business enough to do the work. You like the sound of it. You like the image of being a CEO, but you're not interested in the day-to-day labor involved in building something of your own. Maybe you'd rather show up at eight, leave by five, and not think about work again until the next morning. Maybe you don't want to carry the ultimate responsibility for a business's wins and losses on your shoulders. Whatever the reason for your laziness in launching your business, set yourself free. You can let go of your attempts at entrepreneurship, forget about building an empire, and move on with your life, knowing that being an employee is what you really want.

Anyone who wants it and is willing to work for it can develop the skills and habits necessary to succeed in business. But building a business isn't for everyone. It sounds impressive to say you want to be an entrepreneur and even more so to say you're an empire builder, but when push comes to shove, you have to be willing to put in the work and own the results. So many people sit on ideas while time passes them by and, all around them, other people take action to see if their ideas can actually succeed. Year after year, the folks in that first group talk about the business they want to start, but nothing happens. They find every excuse not to take action, and usually, they blame it on someone or something else. Maybe they're just too scared.

When you really want to start a business, when you're driven to succeed, you find a way to get it done. If you've done the research, you have the know-how, and you have the money you need to launch, but you're still waiting, then you're either lazy, you have no real interest in running a business, or you don't really believe in your business idea or your ability to make it a reality. Fear and doubt can kill your progress, but taking fast action will help you push forward. The faster you move the faster you can figure out what works and what doesn't.

I have no problem getting out there and going after an opportunity because I have the desire to produce wealth. That won't come from me just sitting back and waiting for things to happen. Taking fast action in business means being aggressive. It means thinking faster and being bolder. When you're aggressive, you focus on outpacing the next person at every opportunity. You strive to be smarter strategically, stronger financially, and faster at making decisions and getting things done. Ideally, I want to come into a good business before my partners do. I want to get out of a bad business sooner than the rest of the people in my industry. I want to make more money than my competition and parlay that success to expand my empire. In order to do all of that, I have to move quickly to attack every angle and make sure I have the advantage. If you want to succeed in business, you need to embrace that aggressive side of you and move.

Monetize your gifts—and the gifts of others.

Is your goal to make money or to spend all day following a passion whether it makes money or not? Popular wisdom will tell you to find your passion and the money will follow, but I have a different perspective. Instead, I tell people to follow their gifts. You can be passionate about a lot of things. That doesn't mean you're necessarily good at them, that you want to do them for a living, or that they're the best way for you to make the kind of money you want to earn.

Rather than getting caught up in trying to make your passion your career, I suggest you use your gifts to make money and build a business. We all have a unique set of talents and gifts, and fortunately, you don't have to spend a lot of time trying to identify yours. You already know what your gifts are. Your gifts are the things you do that come easily and naturally to you. When you use your gift, you're in the flow. Even when you're hard at work, it doesn't feel like you're working hard. Your gift is what you do naturally, effortlessly, but which allows you to have great impact. It's often something you take for granted. It comes so easily that you might think it's common sense or just not very valuable. You may not recognize how you can use your gift to make money yet, but there's always a way.

Your gift and what you think of as your passion may overlap or intersect, and if they do, then it makes sense to pursue that passion in some way. But sometimes they'll be completely different, and that's okay. Sometimes, it's better to let your passion be your hobby and use your gift to make a living. Too many people spend a lifetime trying to squeeze a living out of their passions while their God-given gifts go untapped and unexplored. It's a pursuit that leaves them frustrated and broke.

If you're passionate about basketball but your gift is cooking, you might play a pick-up game twice a week, but start a catering company, create a food product line, or build a chain of specialty food stores. If you're passionate about movies but you have a gift for planning and organization, you might launch an event planning company that serves the entertainment industry or get into production rather than screenwriting. When you put your gift to work for you and see the results you can create, you'll find a new kind of passion in that success.

Some entrepreneurs are gifted leaders, talent finders, or team builders. They're gifted at coming up with ideas, creating a plan, or developing innovative marketing strategies. They know how to quickly and easily identify opportunities, even when they don't have a natural gift to execute on them. If any of that sounds like you, then consider how you can use those skills to make the most of other people's gifts. Those capabilities don't come naturally to everyone and, with the right talent on your team, your gifts can give you a serious edge in building almost any kind of business you choose to purse.

When I was growing up, my father had a furniture refinishing business. He wasn't an all-star furniture refinisher, but he was smart enough to hire a couple of talented guys who had the necessary skills to do the work he brought in. The man who runs a commercial cleaning company doesn't necessarily have a gift for making floors shine, and the woman who starts a valet parking business might hate driving. If they're gifted planners, leaders, or marketers, owners can hire team members to do the front-line jobs while they put their own gifts to work managing people or finding new business.

Find the fastest way to the cash.

Too often, entrepreneurs go around and around in circles, trying to figure out how they can do something new and unique to make money. Even when they don't know where to start, they want to be innovative just for the sake of doing something different. They overthink, over-create, and over-deliver. The end result is that they expend too much effort and too much energy, and they put themselves under too much unnecessary stress.

Find the fastest way to the cash. Taking your gifts, your experience, and your network into consideration, how can you quickly start to make a profit? If for example, you already have a reputation or a foothold in a certain industry, it makes sense to exploit that advantage. If you have deep connections in an industry, you need to explore the potential there. Someone with a decade of experience in the classroom could build online courses, create a tutoring service that lets teachers earn extra income, or start a training service for speakers who want to communicate concepts better. All of these will allow that former educator to tap into her network and her experience to get to the money faster.

The fastest way to the cash may not be the opportunity that looks, on the surface, like it would be the most profitable. When I managed talent, my clients were constantly offered opportunities to be spokespeople or partner as the face of a company. It was when they got off brand that they ran into trouble. A tempting proposal from a company that had no relationship to what the client was known for could produce some income, but most of the time, it wasn't going to be the fastest way to the cash or best use of the brand.

I advised entertainers to find ways to grow within the industry first. Performers can create opportunities behind the camera by producing shows and events. A singer who's known for her cutting-edge fashion might partner with a designer. But it doesn't make sense for an on-air fitness personality to launch a luxury jewelry line. She has credibility in the fitness and weight loss industry, but even if she's well known, she'll be starting from scratch, trying to convince people she knows as much about diamonds as she does about diet.

Don't try to innovate when you haven't even begun to exploit what's easily accessible to you. Find opportunities that let you make the most of who and what you already know—and what you're already known for.

Start the clock and keep it running.

Every venture needs a specific deadline by which it will succeed or shut down. Before you launch, decide how long you'll give your new business or a new project within your existing business to become profitable. Identify exactly how much money you'll have to bring in, by what date. Commit to taking the L and moving on to the next thing if you don't hit those numbers. It's a given that some businesses will fail. You don't want to be stuck for years, beating your head against the wall, trying to make something work, when you could be creating success elsewhere.

Years ago, I took over management of an event, and I discovered that it had never been profitable in its ten years of existence. It wasn't paying off, but previous managers had let it ride because it was popular and drew large numbers of people. After a look at the numbers, I made a decision to shut down the existing event and replace it with something different. The new venture still provided plenty of exposure for the brand, but even more importantly, it was profitable right out of the gate.

Numbers don't lie. A business is either profitable or it's not. You either have a clear and executable plan to make it profitable or you don't. I have no problem closing down a losing venture because I know there's always another opportunity out there. I'd rather commit my resources to something that will make money.

Obviously, you don't need to have immediate success to choose to keep your business going. However, you do need to know what success looks like for you and commit to that standard. Answer the following questions to set your personal bar for business success.

1. How much profit does your business need to make in order for you to consider it a success?
2. How long will you give yourself to hit those numbers or close down the business or line of business?
3. And if you do have to shut the doors on your business, what's your next step?
4. Will you have assets you can sell off?
5. Will there be money left to invest in the next opportunity?

The prevailing wisdom from other experts is to give your business a time frame of three years to succeed. I say there's no reason you should keep putting your time and your money into something that hasn't turned a profit in eighteen months and has no *immediate* probability of becoming profitable. Don't get so caught up in ego or the success you fantasize about that you keep throwing away your money and time.

If you're not making money, what you have isn't a business. It's an expensive hobby. If you haven't found a way to turn a consistent profit after a year and a half, get out. You might not be able to recoup your total investment, but it's time to surrender. Shutting it down doesn't mean you failed at business; it just means that particular business failed. Take what you learned from that venture and apply it to the next one.

Rookie Action Steps

1 What? And by when? Create a plan that lays out all of the steps you need to launch your business and make it profitable. Assign a due date to each step and identify who (you or a team member) will be responsible for it. Visit www.GeraldWashington.com/EmpireEssentials to download a free business plan template.
2 What's the next most important action you need to take to launch or grow your business—just one thing? If you've created a plan, you should know what it is. Do you need to find a location, source a product, hire a web designer? Identify that step, and take it.
3 Make a list of your passions, and beside that list, make a list of your gifts. Give yourself permission to let any passions unrelated to your gifts be hobbies you enjoy in your off time. For now, are you using your gifts in your business or the business you plan to build? If not, how can you alter your course to move in that direction? If so, identify more ways you can use your gifts to grow your business faster.

Veteran Action Steps

1. Whether you started your business with a solid plan or somehow stumbled through without one, you can and should create a plan for your next steps. What do you need to learn about the marketplace? How can you continue to grow your business? How will you be prepared to take advantage of the next opportunity? How will you go from business owner to empire builder? What's your exit strategy?
2. Get serious about those ideas you've been considering. Identify one opportunity to scale your business, reach a new audience, or otherwise increase your cash flow. Set a specific deadline by which you'll either move forward or let the idea go and stop messing around with it. Note: If you're not considering any opportunities for growth right now, you're probably not a veteran—or you haven't learned how to think like an empire builder yet.
3. Make a list of your gifts, the things you do naturally well. Spend a couple of days using a time tracker to record how you spend your work days. Assess how much of your time you spend operating in your gifts and how much you spend doing other things. Identify the responsibilities you should hand off to an employee or partner and make it happen.

So how do you do it all? My short answer is this. *You just do it.*

3
Your Empire: It's about Time

Running a business isn't so much about the traditional work-life balance as it is about designing your work and your life so they serve each other. My work creates opportunities for my family and me, and the time I invest in taking care of myself and strengthening important relationships makes me better at what I do. My family gives me a higher purpose for building an empire, but if I never see the people I care about most, I cheat myself as much as I cheat them. If you want to move beyond working for a paycheck or finally stop killing yourself to make a profit out of your business, you have to master your time. There's no way around it.

Money you can always get more of, but time is your one finite resource. When you're slow to take action or you let opportunities pass you by, that time when you could have been increasing your income, building an empire, and creating the life you want for yourself and your family still passes by. Once that time is gone, it's gone. Remember: while you can get rich quickly, it takes time to become wealthy. Yet, time alone won't create wealth for you. How you choose to spend your time will determine whether or not you ever achieve what you set out to do. Making the most of your time means you can never use a lack of time as an excuse for why you're not hitting your goals.

Be conscious of how you spend every hour.

Running a business can easily eat up all of your available time, especially if you also have a family to take care of and spend time with or you still have a full-time job working for someone else. So how do you do it all? My short answer is this. *You just do it.* That might sound dismissive, but it boils down to the reality that you and I have the same twenty-four hours in a day that Sean Combs, Elon Musk, and Oprah Winfrey have. It's easy to explain away their productivity and their achievements by saying they have the money to pay people to do things for them. They absolutely do, but hiring help or bringing on a team doesn't exempt anyone from doing the work it takes to build a business from the ground up. Choose to use your time to get closer to your dream of running a successful business.

Don't get caught up in the kind of busy work that feels like building a business but doesn't bring in the money. You can have a huge social media presence, but can you sell your followers anything? You might be the person everyone in your city knows because you show up at every networking event, but do you have a plan

Don't get caught
up in busy work
that feels like
building a business,
but doesn't
bring in money.

for converting some of those people you shake hands with into clients, ambassadors, or partners? There are lots of great-looking websites out there that aren't making a dime. Those things have their place, but especially in the beginning, your focus should be on income-producing activities.

When you value every hour and consciously choose how you spend it, you no longer feel pulled to waste your time liking and posting everything your friends share on social media. You don't feel obligated to go to every party or hang out with people who have nothing better to do with their time. Instead, you're strategic about planning your rest and relaxation. I don't come home from work, drop down on the couch, and play video games. I plan to use my leisure time for the things I care about. I have a few television shows I like to watch, but I don't report to the TV on Thursday nights at nine o'clock. I fit those shows into my day on Sundays, when I can take the day off and do some binge watching.

Be honest with yourself about how you're spending your time. My wife never lets me forget that sleep is a necessity, but when you're not sleeping, what are you doing with the other sixteen to seventeen hours of your day? If you're spending time on activities that don't directly benefit your family, your business, or you, then you can't complain that you don't have time to work on your business.

Say yes to more.

I don't believe in saying no to an opportunity just because you don't have time to move on it. I believe, one hundred percent, that it's possible to say yes one hundred percent of the time. In my experience, there's always a way to make time. You can innovate, delegate, outsource, or partner with someone to get the job done. If you paint houses, you might have to hire a team of temp workers or subcontract a job to complete a big project. If you're a salon owner, you might need to open your doors on Sundays and Mondays for a period of time. If you sell T-shirts, you might need to find a new printer who can do rush orders. Assume you can get the job done, and then find a way to do it. Sometimes you have to get creative. You have to innovate and do things in a way they haven't been done before.

I credit much of my success in television to the fact that I came from a completely different professional background. I didn't bring the typical expectations to producing TV shows. I didn't know how things were usually done, so I didn't place any limits on the way I did things as an executive producer. Nobody in the industry was shooting on the weekends, for example, but that's what we decided to do. It allowed us to produce more shows than we ever could with a strict weekday shooting schedule. By giving the same crew the chance to work on each show, we created a win-win. The team won because they had a chance to earn more money and get more production credits. We won because, from show to show, we worked with the same team. There was no need to get used to new personalities or train new people to do things our way. Our team knew us and our expectations, and because we were loyal to them, they were loyal to us in return.

Sometimes the only way to get everything done is to delegate. If you don't have employees yet, let technology work for you with online calendars, scheduling apps, and other available automation. When you're ready, you can consider hiring help. Depending on your business, you might want to start by hiring an assistant or several virtual assistants with different skill sets. You might decide to bring on interns to work in your business to handle things like social media and online marketing.

Assume you can get the job done, and then find a way to do it.

There's always a way to get more done, but you can't expect to do it all yourself. Having an innovative mindset has allowed me to figure out how to say yes to more opportunities. I don't believe in letting checks go, and neither should you. Find a way to take advantage of opportunities when they come along.

Prioritize based on your values.

Prepare yourself for the fact that your business will take up a lot of your free time. In fact, if you let it, a business can take over your entire life. When you work for yourself, you can easily find yourself working around the clock. There's always another idea to test, another deal to be made, another connection that could potentially skyrocket your sales or expand your offerings. Especially in the startup phase, it can be tempting to do nothing but work, but that's not sustainable. It's also not fair to the people who are closest to you to give everything you've got to the business.

My wife and my daughters are my top priorities. There's no confusion about how I'll spend any free time I have. They come first because I'm clear about what I value most in my life. Yes, I work a lot, but when I'm with my family, I want to be fully present for them. In the past, I've taken off a month in the summers to spend with my family, and in the near future I look forward to taking off two months every year. As you start and grow your business, you need to have clarity about what you value. Otherwise, work will easily consume all of your time and energy. Don't allow other people or things to set your priorities for you. You decide what people and events deserve your time.

Rookie & Veteran Action Step

1. Are you giving your business enough time? Or has your business taken over your life? Whether you're ready to go from employee to entrepreneur or from entrepreneur to empire builder, you need to make time to do it. You also need to factor in your physical, mental, and spiritual wellbeing, and your most important relationships.
2. For the next week, track how you spend all of your time. Make note of how much time you spend watching TV, scrolling through social media, or otherwise wasting time. Decide what you can eliminate and how you can better spend that time in service of your business.
3. Note how often you make time to work out, give the people who matter most your undivided attention, and engage in your chosen spiritual practice. Make a decision to prioritize the things that mean the most outside of work and add them to your schedule so you can be sure they happen.

4

Your Empire: It's about Money

Recently, my wife and I decided to dramatically downsize from our sprawling home to a large apartment. While I see it as a way of humbling myself so that God doesn't have to do it for me, it's also an opportunity. Every dollar we save can be invested in growing our businesses. Rather than continue to pay for way more square footage than we need, for a house we'll never own, we're making what some people might consider a short-term sacrifice for some serious long-term gains. For us though, it doesn't feel like a sacrifice at all. Building an empire requires you to make smart decisions now so you can have more opportunities later. I'm happy to do that.

Business is the game of money. Wins and losses are measured by the bottom line. When you apply some basic principles of good money management, you give your business a much better chance of thriving and growing. It's the only way you can expect to make enough

You don't connect with a market by giving people what they need. You connect by offering what they want.

money to stay out of the role of employee. Money-management skills are also essential to your success in going from entrepreneur to empire builder. It's hard to develop new lines of business when your first business is in the red.

Minimize expenses.

When I first started in business, I didn't give much of thought to keeping costs in check. I focused more on bringing in as much cash as possible. Like my marketing company, our real estate business did very well from the start, and it grew consistently for four good years. As the money came rolling in, I didn't just want to experience that success as numbers on a bank statement. It was also incredibly important to me to have tangible proof of my achievements and to project an image of success. I was so excited about looking larger than we were that I made bad money decisions. During a time when the real estate market was about to go over a cliff, banks were closing their doors, and the Great Recession was just around the corner, I decided we needed to move to a larger office. Even though I definitely didn't need to hire more people in that moment, I took our five employees and moved them to a bigger office with ten desks.

The collapse of the real estate market wiped out a lot of businesses, but entrepreneurs like my wife, who had spent more modestly and kept expenses to a minimum, lasted a lot longer than I did. I had no reserve to fall back on, and my overhead was much higher than it needed to be. Would my business have shut down even if I'd stayed in my smaller office and kept expenses low? Maybe. Probably. But I would've had more options. I could have bought myself more time to make decisions about how to get out of a bad situation. Instead, the decisions were made for me.

Unnecessary spending is clearly not an investment in your business. An investment is something you expect to give you a return. In other words, by spending that money, you can reasonably expect to increase your profits. Some expenses, like taxes, insurance, and office equipment are absolutely necessary, but you still need to manage your money to minimize your tax burden, avoid carrying unnecessary insurance, and buy the office equipment you need, rather than what you think will impress people. You need a lawyer to review your contracts, but you probably don't need the attorney with the biggest name and the highest fees in your city. Minimize those expenses that won't give you a return in productivity, profitability, or efficiency.

Some expenses, like marketing, should be treated as investments in your business. You spend that money because it increases your ability to earn money. But you still need to make smart decisions and spend only what makes sense for your bottom line. It makes sense to spend money to get your brand in front of the right buyers, but there are limitless ways that you can do that and some cost more than others. Make smart spending decisions based on your business's needs, not your wants or what you see other owners doing.

Know your market.

My wife has a highly engaged and responsive online audience. When she sets out to write a new book, create a course, or deliver a speech, it's incredibly easy for her to find out what her market wants. All she has to do is ask the people in her Facebook group, on her email list, or at live events. She listens to their questions and concerns, and then she creates content and products that respond to their needs and desires. Because she's continually interacting with her audience, she's very clear about what they want.

In entertainment, we relied on formal focus groups to tell us what the market wanted. Television programs can cost from hundreds of thousands on up to millions of dollars to produce, so production companies want to have a good handle on what the audience wants from a show. In that case, it's worth the cost of focus groups and market research to try to create a show that viewers will respond to. However, in your business, you don't have to spend a lot of money to discover what your market wants.

Start by clearly identifying your target market. Are you selling to forty-year-old mothers or young men fresh out of college? What is it they want from a product or service like yours? Whether you're selling books, cars, houses, or events, those two groups will likely be looking for very different things. You have to know who you're selling to before you can understand what they want and how to reach them.

Once you've identified your target market, ask them what they want. You don't need to hire a focus group company or spend a lot of money to do market research. Call up ten of your friends—not just random people, but friends who fit your market profile. Ask them about where they spend their money now. What do they want more of? What would they change about the products they currently buy? What are they looking to purchase but can't find in the marketplace? You can have a bunch of friends over for dinner and have a casual discussion to understand the way they view a product like yours.

Even if you don't have friends in your target market, it's easier than ever to get inside the mind of your target customer. You can ask questions wherever your audience hangs out online. People share a lot of their personal business, including their problems, preferences, and spending habits on social media. It's a great place to do market research. If you belong to an organization that caters to your audience, tap into that resource. You don't have to invest a lot of money in market research, but you will have to invest some time. That being said, be careful not to get so caught up in research that whatever opportunity you were considering passes you by. Remember that one of the principles of business success is to take fast action. Find out what your market wants, and move on to the next step in the process.

Give the market what it wants.

Once you understand your market, their likes and dislikes, their desires and their preferences, *give them what they want.* There's a big difference between needs and wants. You don't connect with a market by giving people what they need. You connect by offering what they want. Of course, your product or service might provide what your customers need, but that's not what they're buying. You should sell them what they want because you won't have to create a desire for it.

When I started promoting parties, I didn't sell teenagers a safe place to spend Friday nights, which they might have needed but weren't thinking about at all. I sold them an opportunity to have fun, a chance to see and be seen and dance to the latest music, something to talk about on Monday when they got back to school—all in a safe place to spend Friday night. Getting what they needed was incidental.

I discovered the benefits of giving the market what it wants when I started my first business in elementary school. On Wednesdays, I'd walk from school to my dad's house, and every time, I'd stop by Ms. Wilson's house to buy candy from her store. All the kids held back a little from our lunch money to buy from her, and I quickly realized that, just like I did, the rest of the student market wanted to eat candy every day, not just when their parents bought it for them.

If I could cut off some of those kids on their way to Ms. Wilson's or sell to them at lunchtime, then I could put some of their money in my pocket. I started selling candy from my backpack, which turned a nice little profit for a kid that age. Later, in high school, I sold candy on a larger scale. A friend's family owned a grocery store, and every Monday, I'd go with them to a wholesaler, where I bought the candy I sold out of my locker during the school day. I paid $8.75 a box for Sour Powers, and I made $30 or $40 on each box.

Since I was breaking the rules by running a business inside the school, small things I could carry made the best products to sell. Of course, older students had interests that went beyond candy, and I started selling other things, like the knock-off Tommy Hilfiger and TAG Heuer watches I bought in L.A.'s downtown garment district. I was a star football player, so a lot of people knew me, and it didn't take long for word to spread about my watch business. I carried men's styles and women's styles, and I could size a watch to fit your wrist. I had a generous return policy, and if the watch you bought from me broke, I'd swap it for a new one. Even teachers started to buy watches from me, and I had a boom in sales when Christmas rolled around and people bought watches to give as gifts. When it was all said and done, I made over $10,000 selling watches at school, and I used $4500 of that money to buy my first car, a black Volkswagen Jetta.

From selling candy to making thousands of dollars selling watches, as a kid I created small businesses that put substantial amounts of money in my pocket for those phases of my life. I did it by understanding what the people around me wanted and giving it to them. *Trying to educate people into wanting what you have to offer is a waste of time.* Instead, understand your market, and then create and promote experiences, products, and services to give them what they already want.

Maximize customer lifespan.

I started throwing high school parties while I was in college because the teenage interns who worked with me had nothing to do on the weekends. But as they aged out of high school, I didn't want to lose that revenue. The interns who hung out at my office and handed out flyers for the parties were going to college, and my theory was that if I could capture you as a freshman in high school, I'd have you as a customer for at least eight years. If you loved my parties when you were a high school student, you'd recognize my brand on a college party and choose to spend your time and money there.

I added college parties and then twenty-one-and-over parties to the list of events I offered. Doing so allowed me to maximize the lifespan of my customers from the four years of high school to eight years or more. And of course, the beginning of that funnel, which started in ninth grade, continued to feed me new customers year after year.

When you're trying to grow your business, your first thought might be how you can get more customers. That makes sense. You want more people to buy your products and services. However, maintaining the customers you already have by giving them more to buy from you is just as important as, and often easier than, adding new customers. If you've done your job, these are people who already know, like, and trust your brand. If loyal customers have to choose between buying from you and buying from another vendor, you will win. Give them reasons to love your brand, and then give them more reasons to give you their money.

Grow your business more slowly

than you think you should.

When my real estate business took off, I had visions of growing it into a Fortune 500 company so I could live out my lifelong dream. (I'd wanted to be CEO of a Fortune 500 company for as long as I could remember.) We were thriving, and for me that meant it was time to expand. Patrice and I had partnered in our real estate ventures, and we had offices in an executive suite building, in Manhattan Beach, California. As the market was tanking, I not only upgraded our office to a bigger space but also invested more revenue back into the business. The sky was falling, and I was clueless.

It's tempting to take short-term success as a sign that your business is ready to grow, but it's a huge mistake. If I had moved more slowly, I would've been able to maintain larger cash reserves. I would've had lower overhead and less debt, and recovering from the setback would have been easier. Having enough demand for growth in the moment isn't enough reason to jump into an expansion, invest in more infrastructure, or bring on new team members. You need enough sustained demand to justify that growth over the long term.

If you're a barber with a small shop, for example, and you're thinking of moving to a bigger, more expensive space, you need to do an honest assessment of your business first. Have you been bursting at the seams for more than a year, or are you overly excited because your business picked up for the holidays? Do you have the volume to support a ten-chair barber shop right now, or are you just in love with the idea of looking like a mogul? Will your current clientele follow you to the new location, and if you think so, how can you be sure? How will you market your business to keep those extra chairs filled all year round? How much will your overhead increase if you move to the bigger shop? What new expenses might come along with the new space? How many barbers do you need to have paying full monthly rent in order to cover those expenses? How will the move affect your profit margin?

In a case like that, I'd recommend you try growth options that require less commitment first. Extend your business hours. Rearrange your current space to add one extra chair and see how that goes. Track the numbers for several months to see where the demand rises and falls. Take small steps to see if your customer base can support the growth you want to see over the long haul.

As you draft your business plan, include some benchmarks for growth so you don't get ahead of yourself. If you're thinking of renting office space, how much consistent monthly profit do you need to be making to demonstrate the ability to pay for that space? If you want to hire your first employees, what kind of numbers do you need to justify them? Never spend just because that's what the next guy is doing, because you want to look bigger than you are, or because you're anticipating an increase in business that may not actually happen. When you think you're ready to grow your business, make the numbers prove it, not just once but over time, before you pull the trigger.

Rookie Action Step

1 Have you taken time to create a business budget yet? Don't just estimate or make up numbers. Do your research, and be realistic about the costs you expect to incur.

Veteran Action Step

1 Take a hard look at your business budget. Identify where you can cut expenses to have cash on hand to take advantage of the next opportunity. Make those cuts, and rather than spending the money elsewhere or giving yourself a raise, save to invest in your next opportunity.

We chase purpose, not money.

– Patrice Washington, America's Money Maven and my wife

5

Your Empire: It's about People

Growing up, my experiences as the captain of my football teams helped me to develop my natural leadership abilities, and those same skills served me well at work. When I worked for Taco Bell as a high school student, I was one of the youngest employees, but I was able to easily motivate my co-workers to meet and exceed our goals. I knew what they cared about most and what incentives I could offer them to get more out of them. Something as simple as taking on a tough job so the other employees could do something easier inspired them to give a higher performance. I mopped the floor and took out the trash, so they didn't have to do it. I took over the deep fryer, a hot greasy job, and let the person assigned to that station spend the day boxing food. I didn't mind working hard, and with everyone in a better mood and feeling appreciation for the way I treated them, the store ran more smoothly.

When I started working in the restaurant, customer service was slow and complaints were high. The store constantly had lines out the door. My co-workers never had any sense of urgency. It was just a paycheck to most of them, and they saw no reason to do any more than the bare minimum required to hold on to their jobs. However, it didn't take long for me to find those ways to organize and motivate them so we could get the food out to customers faster. The store's numbers went up, and even though the company wouldn't give me a management salary at such a young age, I was placed in a management position. The general manager gave me the title, and along with that role came the opportunity for more leadership experience.

Unfortunately, as I grew in my career and launched my own businesses, I started to lose sight of some of the values that had made me a great boss in those early days of my work experience. My wife has since helped me learn a life-changing lesson. *We chase purpose, not money.* As my real estate business grew, I had gotten that backwards. I'd made material gain my single measure of success. That kind of thinking caused me to mistreat team members, overlook flaws in partnerships, and make hiring decisions that didn't always serve me well.

I've since relearned what I always instinctively knew—*other people are always essential to the success of every entrepreneur and empire builder.* It may look like that mogul on the cover of your favorite business magazine did it all alone, but it's just not possible. Even if you never hire an employee or take on a business partner, relationships will make or break your business. Strategic partners, vendors, sub-contractors, distributors, referrals, team members, clients, and customers—without people, you don't have a business. You cannot win in business without applying essential people principles.

Act from integrity.

Making the most of your business relationships requires you to hold yourself to a high standard of integrity. Remember the story I shared earlier in this book about running the cookie business in my high school? I got burned on that deal because, even after I committed to my principal that the proceeds would go to the school, I thought I could walk away with all the money. If that had been a serious business deal in my adult life, I would've burned a bridge with a potential partner. He would've been unlikely to do a deal with me in the future or to refer any business my way. I got exactly what I deserved. I walked away with nothing in my pocket from the cookie business, but I took something much more valuable out of that deal. It was one of the first in a series of lessons that taught me the true value of integrity in business.

As a young entrepreneur, I didn't fully get what it meant to run a business with integrity. Even in my twenties, when I was in the real estate business, I was more focused on making sure everyone on my team knew who the boss was, and I sometimes failed to treat them the way I'd want a boss to treat me. When I had other things going on, I'd pay employees late and think nothing of it. Still, they did what I told them to, and because they did, I convinced myself that they all respected me. Later, I found out they pretended to respect me to my face so they could hold on to their jobs, but they complained about me behind my back. They didn't feel like I cared about them, and they reacted accordingly.

As I matured, and especially after suffering serious losses in business and in life, I realized that there is no gray area when it comes to integrity. It means keeping your word, honoring your commitments, paying people on time or being straight with them about why you can't, and treating everyone you interact with fairly.

I've seen people at every level of business renege on deals and break promises. While they may experience a short-term win and may even look like success stories, those actions have consequences. They're destroying relationships with people who could potentially help them achieve even greater success in the future. They're developing a reputation as untrustworthy and strictly out for self. They're creating an environment in which everyone around them feels like they have to get theirs at any cost. As a result, there's no loyalty on either side of the table.

Recently, I left a project which meant leaving behind the team I'd pulled together there. Tanya, Terrell, Ruben, and Jennifer had been devoted and hard-working, and I would miss working with them. When I took the team out for a goodbye dinner, they were shocked and sad to see me go. There was nothing but respect and appreciation on both sides of the table, and this time, I had no doubt that it was all genuine. I didn't take any pleasure from their disappointment, but I did appreciate the fact that it meant I had done my job well. I had taken the lessons I'd learned and become the kind of leader who inspired them to give their all every day. I had treated them as my partners, rather than as someone there for me to control.

Whether you're dealing with team members, partners, clients, customers, or competitors, the way to win today and over the long haul is to build those relationships on a foundation of integrity. At the end of the day, you know the difference between right and wrong in the way you relate to people. Choose to do what's right.

Don't hire your family.

One of the defensive strategies I mentioned earlier in this book was a "don't do" strategy. *Don't hire your family.* You can probably name all kinds of exceptions, people you know, read about, or see in the media who all seem to run family businesses without any problems. Maybe they actually do, but keep in mind that none of us knows what goes on behind closed office doors or once they get home. You have no idea how that wife-husband or sister-brother team functions at work, what their bottom line looks like, or how working together has affected their relationship. My advice not to hire family comes from personal experience with two of my closest relatives, my brother and my father. Both situations came to bad endings for very different reasons.

My father and I were so close that I never thought working together would be a problem for us, and while the work lasted, it wasn't. After I closed my business in Los Angeles, I still believed I could rebuild with real estate. My dad was my best friend, and I wanted him to share in what I was creating. I encouraged him to retire from his job and come to work for me. Because he believed in me, he left his stable job in Los Angeles and moved to New Orleans. In hindsight, I should've let him believe in me and support me from a distance.

Even as the real estate market started to shut down in Southern California, I still had projects going in New Orleans. I was convinced I could make them profitable, so I went out there on my own before bringing my family along. Rather than spend money I didn't have on a house or an apartment, I lived in the unfinished basement of one of the properties I was rehabbing. Hard money lenders were willing to invest in me, and we survived off that hard money for a while. I had seen how much money real estate could generate and I wanted more of it. Unfortunately, I still didn't understand the big picture of what was going on with the economy. I wanted my dad to be a part of the success I foolishly envisioned for myself, and I brought him into my business. My timing couldn't have been worse.

In the end, there was nothing I could do to make those Louisiana properties profitable. I still didn't have an exit strategy, and once again, I waited too long to get out. I gambled, and I lost. But I had also gotten my father to gamble on me, and my loss was his loss too. He had trusted in my business acumen and expected me to make good decisions, but I hadn't fully vetted the business I got us into. When everything shut down, my dad had to get a job at Lowe's, the hardware store chain, to make ends meet.

While there's nothing wrong with working at Lowe's or any other honest job that pays your bills, my father had left his long-term employment, which certainly paid more than working the front lines of retail, to work with me. I'd really believed I could still make real estate work in New Orleans, but I had been wrong. And my mistake cost my father the security he had enjoyed before he left Los Angeles. I had to live for years with the guilt of knowing I'd put my father in a precarious financial position. I never want to have that kind of experience with a family member again.

Working with my brother was completely different from working with my dad. For one thing, unlike my dad, who had years of entrepreneurial experience and understood the way I worked, my brother was young and untested in the business world. When I brought him on to work as my assistant, I was really trying to save him. I thought I could help him find his place in the world. By the time my brother came to work for me, my family and I had made our move from New Orleans to Atlanta and gotten back on our feet. My brother came to live with us while he figured some things out, and I thought giving him a job made sense for both of us. He'd have a sense of purpose and access to opportunities, and I'd be working with someone who already knew me.

When it came down to it, my vision of the two of us working side by side didn't translate so well into reality. At the time, my brother was too young to make the kind of commitment and put in the long days I expected of anyone who worked with me. Ten years younger than I was, he was in a totally different phase of life.

He couldn't keep up with my pace, and he was unwilling or unable to talk to me honestly about it. Before long, we were at odds, and I had to fire him. Then we had to see each other at home every day with that tension hanging between us like a thick smoke screen we couldn't walk through. No matter how close your relationship is or how much you love each other, that's an uncomfortable position for both people.

My brother now works with me indirectly. In his current position, his success reflects well on me, but I'm not his boss. He's not under my thumb, and I'm not monitoring his actions or writing his paychecks. We work together from a distance, and that shift in our working relationship means that, when he stays with us from time to time, we can focus on hanging out as brothers without any unnecessary pressure or strain.

Taking on your relatives as your employees puts everyone involved in a vulnerable position. They now have to defer to you as the boss at work and try to maintain your existing relationship at family dinners and holiday get-togethers. Your relative is now in a position of vulnerability. You know what kind of worker he is. You know how much she makes, when she gets paid, and where that money comes from. Think about how you would feel if your sister, your brother, or your cousin controlled your paycheck. Think about how that might change the way you talk to each other and the way you make family decisions. When one of you is the boss, your relationship takes on a whole new power dynamic, which can be hard to leave at the office.

Depending on that person's role, your family member might also have access to a lot of information about you, the kinds of details you wouldn't necessarily share with them. Consider this. Do you really want your family to know how much you make on every deal, when your business is skyrocketing and when it's struggling, how much debt you have, or what problems have surfaced in your office?

Any employee-relative you hire will have a difficult challenge to face. At the same time, you'll have the added burden of constantly having to draw the line between the office and home. There's absolutely such a thing as spending too much time together. You're working forty or fifty hours a week in the same office, and then you have to see each other at home or on holidays. Figuring out how to maintain that family relationship while holding your relative to the same standard you would expect any other employee to meet can get complicated. Sometimes, that balance is impossible to maintain. And trust me; there's nothing fun about having to fire someone close to you.

The pressure of knowing your sister or brother, mother or father, aunt, uncle, or cousin depends on you for their livelihood can seem like no big deal when things are going well. But when your business takes a hit, and you see someone you love suffer because of it, you can't help but feel responsible and even guilty. After all, you were the one in charge when things went bad. It's normal to want to take advantage of available help, especially when you're first starting out, and relatives are often willing to give you free or cheap labor for a while. As your business grows and prospers, it's natural to want to offer your family opportunities to be a part of it, but working with your relatives is rarely that simple. Resist those temptations, and find other ways to share your success.

Always be interviewing for your next opportunity.

While I was working for Taco Bell in Atlanta, I received a call from Rushion McDonald, entertainer Steve Harvey's manager. He asked if I wanted to earn some extra money. Rushion was doing a major renovation on his home, and he needed someone to be there to supervise things while he was on the road. I said yes to the offer. There was nothing glamorous about it. I'd be sleeping on his floor and basically serving as security for the property and building supplies. However, it paid more than I was making in fast food, and I was grateful for the chance to earn some extra income. I also believed that, if I made a good impression, Rushion could help me find more work.

One night, Rushion called and asked if I could bring in some flooring that was sitting on an eighteen-wheeler a block away from his home. Left outside, it would swell and be damaged by the Georgia humidity, and he didn't have anyone on site to take care of it. He offered me a thousand dollars to haul it all to the house, and I jumped at the chance. After a seven-to-seven shift at Taco Bell, I was tired, but I was in. It was a chance earn more money, but it also a great opportunity to demonstrate that I was always willing to do more than the bare minimum. Each time I was asked to do something more than I'd been hired to do, I responded with enthusiasm.

I did that job at one hundred fifty percent until the house was finished and Rushion moved into the house. Not long after, he called and offered me a position as the sponsorship coordinator for the Hoodie Awards, later renamed the Neighborhood Awards, a huge annual event. That job allowed me to finally quit Taco Bell for good. My wife and I cried tears of joy as we burned one of my Taco Bell uniforms, knowing we would never put ourselves in that position again. I also kept a uniform and had it framed. It hangs in my office with a plaque that reads, "This time in my life taught me humility."

Sponsorship coordinator may sound like a big title, but it wasn't a prestigious position. In fact, a lot of people who came through the office looked at me like I was a peon. I didn't care what they thought. I paid attention to the deals that went down around me, and I learned from the good as well as the bad. I had the consistency of a regular paycheck, and I was one step closer to getting back into business for myself again. I gave a hundred and fifty percent on that job too.

Too often, people become arrogant, even in their mediocrity. They don't want to take on anything outside of their job description. Employees give the minimum they can to get by and maybe qualify for an annual three percent salary increase. Entrepreneurs meet customers' basic expectations but fail to give people any reason to buy from them again. If you really want to succeed in business, if you want to grow from an entrepreneur to an empire builder, you can't afford to fall into that trap. My wife likes to say you never know when someone is watching who has the power to bless you. She's right. Treat everything you do like you're the CEO of that task or that division. You're always interviewing for your next opportunity, and you need to treat every account, every client, every customer, every vendor, and everyone you interact with accordingly.

Build and leverage relationships.

When I sold watches in high school, I purchased from the same vendors over and over. It didn't take long to build relationships with them, and because of that, I was able to negotiate better prices and increase my profit margin. It was an early indicator of the power of relationships, and experience has shown me that relationships matter in every aspect of business.

My father and my uncle weren't business partners. They each owned their own independent businesses. However, because they had complementary services and a good relationship, they were able to form an informal partnership. Uncle Tabb owned an upholstery business, and my father's company refinished furniture. They took advantage of the opportunity to partner on projects or share customers.

Now that I'm living in Southern California again and getting back into that real estate market, I'm approaching it differently. For one thing, I'm developing bigger, multi-unit residential properties and commercial properties. I'm also leveraging my relationships in new ways. Instead of thinking I know everything, I've partnered with someone who understands the L.A. market as it is today. There are countless ways to leverage the relationships you have with people, especially other business owners, decision makers, and influencers. Handing out business cards isn't relationship building. It's not enough to just build your network. Instead, make those connections and then constantly look for opportunities to make those relationships work for both parties.

Embrace competition.

When I went into the real estate business the first time around, I partnered with the woman who would later become my wife because we had skill sets that would complement each other. Patrice already had a broker's license and real estate experience, and I had the marketing know-how. It was a perfect fit, especially since I had no desire to go through the broker licensing process. I had never tested well, and I knew I didn't want to put myself through the real estate exam. By partnering with her, I could exploit the booming real estate market without having to sell real estate myself. I grew the business by going hard with our marketing.

In any industry, the majority of the players will copy each other's marketing strategies. If it works—or even looks like it works—for one company, others will jump on the bandwagon and do more of the same. At that time, yellow-and-black real estate signs were big in our area, so much so that the color combination became associated with homes for sale. Rather than follow suit, I decided to take what the competition was doing and amplify it. I had our cargo vans painted yellow and wrapped with yellow-and-black graphics. Other agents had bright signs sitting in yards, but our vans were like moving billboards. They were a lot bigger than the yard signs, and they drove all through the city, maximizing our exposure.

Rather than look at your competitors in your industry as a threat, look to them for inspiration. They can be the starting point for you to do things differently. They can motivate you to set higher goals for your business because if they're achieving big things, so can you. They can push you to put in a little more effort because you see how their efforts are paying off for them. Let the businesses in your niche challenge you to do more in your industry. Let the top performers set an example for you to follow and exceed. Learn from what they've done well, and then see what you can do differently or better.

As executive producer of *Steve*, the daytime talk show, I could easily have looked at similar shows as the enemy. Instead, when we premiered, I looked at *Ellen* as a model. She had already been in that space, and doing well, for years. I had my team assess the way they did things on her show and emulate what they did best. We didn't need to reinvent the wheel. We learned from existing best practices.

To run your life or your business by reacting to someone else's strategies is a losing game. Instead, look at your competitors as models of what you can do or as an opportunity for what you can do better. In some cases, you may even be able to partner on deals with businesses that seem like they should be your competition. You can't escape competition because you'll never find a field that has no one else in it. When MySpace launched, in 2003, the company pretty much had the social networking arena to itself, but that quickly changed. Any industry with potential for profit will draw new people launching new businesses. It's your job to embrace that competition and use it to your advantage.

Rookie & Veteran Action Step

1 Identify your biggest competitors and figure out what they're doing well right now and where they're missing the mark. How can you take similar strategies and do them even better or in new, innovative ways? What are your competition's weaknesses? How can you be strong where your biggest competitors are weak?

Do you have
a contract?

6
Your Empire: It's about the Deal

I didn't go to Occidental College to try to earn a 4.0, to be the best student, or to go on to get a doctorate and spend my life in academia. Education was important to my family. My father didn't finish college, but my mother earned a master's degree, and they both saw higher education as the path to prosperity. Of the colleges that accepted me, Occidental was the most prestigious, and a few of my friends were going there to play football, so that's where I chose to go. I decided to attend the private college with a tuition price tag of $36,000 a year (and no scholarships for football), but realistically, community college or a state university would've been a much better fit for me and would've saved me tens of thousands of dollars in student loans. Some people love learning for its own sake, but I wasn't that kid. I went to college to make my parents proud and to gain the knowledge I'd need to maximize my earning potential and propel my career to new heights.

The high school GPA that got me into college was more a result of my status as a football star than my academic prowess. Once I started college, my grades fell way off, but I pushed through. I chose to study economics, but I really didn't understand the purpose of that major or what kinds of jobs it would lend itself to after I graduated. I had no desire to work on Wall Street or to spend my days sitting in a cubicle putting together actuarial tables. I didn't want to go out and get a good government job either. For as long as I could remember, since before I even understood what it meant, I'd wanted to be my own boss and eventually become the CEO of a Fortune 500 company. Fresh out of high school, I thought majoring in economics was the same thing as studying business, which it wasn't. However, I also minored in psychology, and that study allowed me to better understand the way people think, the way they make decisions, and what motivates them. That knowledge has been invaluable to me, especially when it comes to negotiating deals.

In business, almost everything is, or can be, a negotiation. The price you charge for your services, the salary you pay an employee, the commission you get on sales, bulk rates for supplies and products, office lease terms, and more. It can all be negotiated. Because it's such an integral part of doing business, you cannot become a successful entrepreneur without understanding how to negotiate the best deal possible. If this isn't your strong point yet, then make it a priority to master the skill. The more you practice the principles of winning negotiation, the better you'll get at it. Every deal, every negotiation, is a chance for both sides to win or lose. Your goal in every negotiation should be for everyone involved to walk away feeling like a winner.

To be successful in negotiations of any kind you need to follow a few guiding principles:

1. Know what you want and who you're negotiating with.
2. Know what they want and be able to give them most of it.
3. Define your deal-breakers.
4. Keep your alternatives and theirs in mind.
5. Negotiate for long-term success.
6. Get every deal in writing.

Know what you want and who you're negotiating with.

Waiting on the person on the other side of the table to tell you what you can get from the deal is a rookie mistake. Even if they seem to be more than willing to share a full menu of what they can offer, there's a better than average chance that they're not telling you everything you could get from the deal. The only way you'll know for sure is to do your homework and analyze all aspects of the transaction.

Show up to every negotiation with a clear understanding of all of the variables of the deal. Do your research. If you're renting office space, for example, you should know what comparable properties are leasing for, but there's a lot more involved in that transaction than just the monthly rent. Other variables, like the length of the lease term, cancelation clauses, and who pays for repairs and improvements, all need to be considered in the deal. You can't know what you want until you know everything involved in the transaction.

It's just as important to understand who you're dealing with in every transaction. The bigger the deal the more information you should have about the person you're dealing with. If at all possible, talk to other people you know who've worked with this person in some capacity and find out about their experience. In most cases, it's easy to do some online research and find out some background information about the person you're dealing with. Do you have any interests, organization memberships, or background in common? What path did he take to reach this position of decision maker? What does she seem to value most and want to achieve for herself and her business? Who does he need to confer with before a final decision is made? The more you know, the more leverage you'll have negotiations.

Define your deal-breakers.

After you've looked at the deal from all angles, decide what aspects are must-have, nonnegotiable, deal-breakers for you. If you're not willing to walk away from the deal over it, then it's not really a deal-breaker. Don't ever give an element of the deal disproportionate importance and make it look like it could kill or make a deal if that's not the case. That can create confusion and cost you a deal you could've made work if you'd been clear.

Most variables will be negotiable in a given deal, but a few will rise to the level of deal-breaker. Start with getting clarity on your business values. Anything that conflicts with your business's values and mission almost certainly worth taking a stand against when you're at the negotiating table. Other things, like vague terms, a refusal to put the deal in writing, and terms that would require you to skirt the law are always unacceptable.

Every time you negotiate, you will have deal-breakers that are specific to that negotiation. It could be price, delivery method, turnaround time, or something else. It's your responsibility to be aware of every aspect of the deal and define your deal-breakers as well as what you're willing to be flexible on or give up completely.

Keep your alternatives—and theirs—in mind.

Never enter into a negotiation without a clear idea of what you'll do if the deal doesn't go through. The better your alternatives, the more strongly you can hold to your position, even on points that aren't actually your deal-breakers but just make for a better deal. You'll be able to take more risks and ask for more of what you want if you know you have someplace else to take your business or a way out of the deal if you need it.

I recently negotiated a real estate deal that required me to put a large sum of money in escrow. My cash was at risk, but before I signed on the dotted line, I wanted to know what my alternatives were. In that case, I called my business partner at the time and asked him what my outs might be. He's an expert on real estate contracts, and he had no problem pointing out clauses I could include that would decrease the chance that I would lose my money if I found out something about the property that made me want to pull out of the deal. By the time he and I finished talking, I had alternatives and could negotiate with confidence.

You also need to find out as much as you can about the alternatives available to the other party. When I negotiated deals with television networks on behalf of Steve Harvey, I made it a point to know what the networks' options were. If the deal fell through, where could they go to get an on-air personality with ratings as high as Steve's and a project ready to go? In most cases, they had few options. Because I knew what the network needed and I knew we were one of the few places they could find it, I could take more risks in negotiating the deal. It was highly unlikely that they'd walk away without trying really hard to reach an agreement and give us most of what we wanted.

Know what they want and be able to give them most of it.

Before you come to the table to negotiate, it's important to get as clear as you possibly can about what the other person or people will want out of the deal. That will give you some leverage—but only if you can actually give them most of it. Before you ever start to hammer out the deal, you should do everything within your power to find out what the other party will want; what their deal-breakers are likely to be; what constraints on money, time, or resources they might be working with; what their short-term and long-term goals are; what kinds of deals they've negotiated in the past; and exactly what you expect them to want from you. Put yourself in the other party's position and make a list of what you think they'll want and what you can give. The bigger or more important the deal is, the more you need to understand the other side.

Even after you've done all your homework, there's still a chance that something unexpected will come up while you're trying to do the deal. That's okay. You'll be prepared to handle it.

Negotiate for long-term success.

In every deal I make, I'm banking on long-term results. Right now, I can buy a single-family, three-bedroom, two-bath home for $75,000. Let's say I put another $75,000 into rehabbing it. In the right area, I can sell that house for $225,000, but that's not my end game. My goal is to then use that $75,000 profit to invest in multi-unit residential properties that will increase my monthly cash flow for years to come.

Every time you negotiate a deal, ask yourself how it fits into your big picture. How will it serve your business in the long run?

How does this transaction fit into your vision for your empire? If you're just going for a quick win, be aware of that and treat the deal accordingly. However, most of the time, whatever you negotiate should move you closer to your long-term goals for your life as an empire builder.

Get every deal in writing.

By the time we started working together, this up-and-coming comedian and I had known each other for a while. If you had asked me, I'd have said, yeah, we were cool. Our paths crossed often, so when he asked me to review one of his contracts, I was glad to share some insights. As a result of that input, he doubled his fees. Not surprisingly, he was happy with that outcome, and we discussed the possibility of an ongoing relationship. I wouldn't touch the projects he'd already booked, but when something new came up, I'd do the negotiating on his behalf. In exchange, he would pay me an agreed upon commission. This was an agreement that truly seemed like a win-win.

The relationship worked well for both of us. I helped him double or even triple his salary on more gigs. In cases where he wasn't even on the radar for the job, I put his name in for consideration, and he expanded his platform. I negotiated on his behalf, and my efforts increased his annual salary by more than three hundred thousand dollars. I also asked for and got him additional perks he hadn't thought to include in his contracts. While the deals only added a small amount to my bank account every month, I was helping a friend build his career, and I felt good about that. Rather than taking a cut off the top of each deal before he was paid, as is common practice, I allowed him to pay me on his schedule. Once a month, he wrote me a check for my commission. Things were going smoothly.

And then, almost overnight, the relationship changed. Our interaction went from friendly to strained. Before I knew it, we were sitting in front of a third-party, who was trying to sort out my client's claim that I'd been overcharging him. I took the charge as a personal insult, and the comedian tried to defend his position. The conversation went from calm to heated until our mediator interrupted with a pivotal question. *"Do you have a contract?"* he asked. We both said no.

The mediator got up and walked out of the room.

The conversation was over just as fast as it had started. He wasn't going to sit there and try to figure out who was telling the truth or where the misunderstanding was. Given what I knew about my client, I could only guess that someone had given him bad information that made him question our deal. Rather than come and talk to me about it, he'd taken action that destroyed any trust we had between us, and in that moment, our working and personal relationships were over.

It doesn't matter if your agreement is for a one-time event or service or an on-going relationship. You need to get *everything* down in writing. Not some things. Not most of it. Every single detail. (My wife, who has always been very good about this, was not happy with me when I shared how things had transpired.) But I like to move fast, and frankly, I allowed the appearance of friendship—and emotion—to take the place of facts and the core business practice that dictates that you should always have a contract. It was a mistake I'd made before, and in the past, it had cost me a lot more money. This broken promise cost me less, but I was finally ready to learn the lesson. *No more deals without written contracts.*

Even though courts might recognize handshake agreements, or oral contracts, it still comes down to your word against the other person's. Without a written agreement, you'd have trouble proving your position. You'd have to prove the terms of the agreement in court, and that can be hard to do. Most often, it won't be worth the time and money required to hire an attorney and fight it out. You're much better served by having a contract drawn up and reviewed by a knowledgeable attorney before you seal the deal. When you're first getting started, that might seem like an unnecessary expense, but the cost on the backend, if things go wrong, can be much higher.

Rookie Action Step

1 Make a list of the basic agreements you'll need to do business. Are there some standard contracts you can purchase and use? Do some research and find out how much it would cost to have these agreements drawn up by and/or reviewed by an attorney.

Veteran Action Step

1 Take a look at your current business relationships. Where are you operating on trust, friendship, or a handshake? Start putting written agreements in place now.

7

Your Empire: It's about Your Impact

It was a warm spring day in Southern California, and I'd decided to take my video conference call from my favorite local café. Sitting on the patio, I had one eye on my laptop. The other was on people watching as I enjoyed the near-perfect weather. As my conference call was ending, a young boy, not more than eight or nine, approached me, and I recognized him right away. I often saw him in the neighborhood, toting around a cardboard box while his grandmother hovered in the background, keeping a watchful eye on him. As he came towards me, he had that cardboard box in his hands.

"Would you like to buy a candy bar?" he asked. He mumbled something about a fundraiser, but I had the distinct feeling that the money would go to help his grandmother pay her bills.

"When you're selling something," I told him, "you should speak up. Speak clearly and look people in the eye."

He looked up at me.

"See. That's better already. When you talk to people, don't hang your head. Now tell me what you're selling again."

I did not want or need a candy bar. However, it was a school night, and I thought about Reagan, back at home with her mother, doing her homework and getting ready for the next day. Her life was one of privilege and comfort compared to this kid's life. I told this young boy that if I paid for the entire box of candy I expected him to go home and do his homework. After a moment of disbelief, he gladly accepted the deal. I handed him a hundred dollars and told him to keep the candy. Even though I was sure he'd be back out selling his candy bars again sometime soon, I was happy to give him one afternoon off from his job. I hoped he could ride his bike or play a game of touch football with his friends. I hoped he'd have one afternoon of just being a kid.

I would always have been happy to talk to that young boy and give him a little advice, but I could never have handed over that money if it was going to take food out of my own children's mouths. Becoming an empire builder has put me in the position to bless other people in ways small and large. Not only can I provide my family with more opportunities, I can also have a positive impact on other folks wherever I go. I can give a few dollars to someone who needs it. My wife and I are now in a position to make significant donations to the causes we believe in. Our success isn't just for us. It will have a ripple effect on the people we care about and our community.

Give back.

Financial contributions are a great way to give back, and you should share your material wealth in the ways that work best for you. But that's not the only way to give back. Often, money isn't even the best way to help people. (My hope is that the advice I gave the little boy trying to be a salesman will take him much farther than the hundred dollars will.) As an empire builder, you'll be in a position to use your money for good, and you should, but you should also do more. When you can, you should help people develop the means to create their own wealth.

Building an empire will require you to have employees, and I can't overstate the importance of creating jobs for people. Not everyone wants to be the owner. There are plenty of qualified, talented people who will forever appreciate the opportunities you give them. Make sure you prioritize the development of your team so they get more from their time with you than just a paycheck.

At the same time, teaching, mentoring, and guiding others along the path to success shouldn't be limited to the people who work for you. There are innumerable opportunities for you to share your expertise. Figure out the platform that works best for you, and then use it. Talk to the young people in your family about what you do and how you do it. Bring on interns who can get school credit for working for you and learn something about business in the process. Establish formal or informal relationships with mentees who want to follow in your footsteps. Speak to large audiences, or write a book. Be confident in your ability to maintain and increase your success even as you teach others to create their own. Teaching someone else how to light a candle doesn't blow yours out. The person you mentor may be your next successful partner.

Leave a legacy.

I lost my father before he could see how I recovered financially, but the legacy he left me with was invaluable. My father taught me to believe in myself and my gifts. He showed me what a strong work ethic looks like, and he demonstrated by example that you never have to rely solely on an employer for your livelihood. He also taught me the importance of family.

As I build my empire, I always have an eye on the future and what it will hold for my family, especially my wife and children. My greatest accomplishment is creating more opportunity for them. My success removes the limitations from my children's lives. It eliminates the limits they might otherwise put on themselves. Because Reagan lives with me, she has the benefit of seeing how I handle business on a daily basis. She knows Daddy does more than one thing, so she's getting an early lesson in diversification and an understanding that she can be accomplished in many different areas. She's learning to think like an empire builder by recognizing her gifts and the wide variety of ways she can apply them. She has learned that she never has to put herself in a box.

My girls are still young, and what they want to be when they grow up is subject to change. That's fine with me. I don't know what paths they'll choose, but I know one thing for sure. As they grow older, I'm proud to be in a position to expose them to more, give them new experiences, and open doors for them that would otherwise remain shut. If Giana wants to be a chef, I can introduce her to innovative chefs and restaurateurs and send her to study at the best culinary schools in the world. If Leila still wants to be a fashion designer, then I can make sure she sees the most creative, cutting-edge fashion shows and learns how to create her own label. And if Reagan still wants to be in business for herself, well, her parents will serve as her first and best coaches and consultants.

My family is my first priority in everything I do. However, the legacy I leave will be comprised of the sum total of the positive impact my businesses will have on the world. This includes my employees who go off and start businesses of their own, using the knowledge they gained while working for me. My businesses provide a broader contribution by enhancing the financial stability of my community. Beyond the jobs we create, we pay taxes that help support the infrastructure at local, state, and federal levels. And like the kid with the candy, we often give to others simply because we feel it is the right thing to do. It's an expression of appreciation for all the blessings we have. At some point, my wife and I will choose specific causes we want to support in a deeper way, but for now, we're grateful to be able to give where and how we choose.

This is the freedom building an empire gives you. The work you put in today and tomorrow will give you financial freedom, and eventually, time freedom. It will open doors that would otherwise remained closed to you and the people in your life. Your empire will have an impact that outlives you.

Rookie & Veteran Action Step

1 What's your vision for your empire? Start with the end in mind and define the empire you want to build *and* the legacy you want to leave. Keep that vision in front of you in whatever form works best for you—a vision board or a list of goals—and work every day to make it a reality.

A Final Word

I'm not delusional. I realize that most people who read this book will never get past the employee stage even though they harbor dreams of running their own business. Those who do step into entrepreneurship will likely get stuck in a position of freelancing or running a mom-and-pop enterprise. That's just what the statistics show. People who want more get stuck at these two levels out of fear. They're afraid to take a risk. They're afraid to face a setback. They're afraid to look stupid. You must have the grit, the fire, and a desire to achieve greatness in order to become a true empire builder. You have to be willing to take the biggest risks if you expect to get the biggest payoff.

If that sounds too scary or like too much work, I wish you well in your other endeavors. But if you have a relentless drive to become an empire builder, I want that for you. I want that for the people around you, and for your community. Do the work. Apply the principles in this book. Find a mentor, or connect with my wife or with me for coaching. You have to be willing to push yourself beyond where you've ever been before. That's how empire builders are made.

I LOOK FORWARD TO SEEING YOU ON THIS JOURNEY!

Gerald Washington @empirebuildergw

CPSIA information can be obtained
at www.ICGtesting.com
Printed in the USA
LVHW040743040919
629882LV00011B/310/P